Day Trading

The Ultimate Detailed Guide for Maximum Profits with Strategies Involving (Investing, Day Trading, Stock Exchange, Risk Management and Trader Psychology)

By

James Stevens

Published by Shepal Publishing

Table of Contents

Introduction

The financial market avails an opportunity for people to make huge profits from already established businesses. Many people who have had a chance to trade in the financial markets are now enjoying great returns, some even on a daily basis. Trading in the stock market can take time, which may not be an option for someone looking for a quick return. Day trading offers an excellent solution, allowing for trading in stock to occur over the period of one day.

As a day trader, you will think differently and critically as this is the only way you will get to make a smart trade that will give you a profit. You will work independently and rely on your personal instincts to make a trade. There is a lot that is involved in day trading but you have to start somewhere, which is why you need this eBook, to pick up some essential tips about day trading before you get ready to start pocketing some profits from it.

This book contains all the information that you need as a beginner to get started in day trading so that you can make some profits. Get ready to learn about the trading strategies that are suitable for day traders so that you can select a strategy that best meets your trading needs. Learn the importance of planning and how it can benefit your trading. Learn great tips that will help you trade like an expert even on your first trades. Start day trading on a high note with guidance from this book.

Chapter 1:
The Basics of Stock Exchange, Investing and Trading

The stock market, which is also called the equity market is a part of the financial market where shares of companies that are publicly held are issued out and traded either through over the counter markets or though exchanges. The market benefits the companies and investors as well; companies enjoy some capital and in return, they give out part of their ownership to people who buy their shares. A small amount of money can transform into a large sum easily through the stock market. Investors on the other hand enjoy the benefit of making some profits from businesses without necessarily going through the hassle of starting up their own business.

Investing and Trading

These are the two ways through which one can benefit from the financial market.

Investing aims at building wealth gradually over an extended period of time. An investor will buy and hold stocks for huge returns at a later date. They increase their profits by reinvesting the small dividends that they receive from their investments. The benefits that investors eye are for instance interests, dividends and also stock splits. You can invest in a certain company for years or decades for long term benefits.

Trading on the other hand involves buying and selling of stocks frequently. It is aimed at benefitting from the small returns that investors do not get to enjoy. Investors will be comfortable with a monthly return of say 10% for instance but traders will always want more, say 15%. Traders capitalize on the market fluctuations in order to enjoy some profits and they buy when the prices are down, then sell when the prices go up. This happens within a very short period of time. Basically, traders are happy with the small but frequent profits that they make every day.

When investors are waiting for less profits every month, investors bear more risks but can make higher profits and other times, losses within a specific period of time. Investors have to be on the lookout for high probability trading setups if they want to make some profits, which does not work all the time.

Trading styles

Understanding the various trading styles is essential for traders, and it refers to the timeframe or the holding period within which a trader will buy and sell his stocks. According to their styles, traders generally fall under four categories:

i)   The position trader whose position is held from months to years for long term returns.

ii)   The scalp trader whose position is held from seconds to minutes. This type of trader does not hold overnight positions.

iii)   The swing trader whose positions are held from days to weeks.

iv)   The day trader whose trading positions are held throughout the day. He does not hold overnight positions too.

This book will help you make excellent returns as a day trader, ensuring that you are able to create and execute a strategy that will lead you to profit.

Chapter 2:
What Day Trading is all About

Buying and selling of a security within a single trading day is what day trading is all about. This strategy is common in the foreign exchange market, also called the forex market and in the stock market as well. Day trading uses high amounts of leverage and only a few smart and short term trading strategies to take advantage of small changes in the price of highly liquid stocks and currencies for a profit. Day trading is crucial in the marketplace and day traders are considered very important for two essential reasons:

1. They keep the market running efficiently through arbitrage

2. They support stock market's liquidity

Who takes part in Day Trading?

There are professional day traders and these are those who are in it for profits. In addition, you will find novice traders that go into day trading as a hobby which means that they are not always focused on the profits. This book shall mainly focus on the professional day traders. These traders are well established in the market and expertly equipped with knowledge and skills on how the market operates in order to always make a smart move. Here are some of the things that makes them successful in day trading:

a) Knowledge: Day traders need to have sufficient knowledge on the market fundamentals in order to succeed in it. One needs to conduct extensive research on how the market operates and how processes fluctuate in the market to be able to make a smart move. Knowledge and great experience in the market will ensure that a day trader is successful.

b) The right strategy: A day trader needs to be really smart to succeed, and to elevate their opportunities they must choose a trading strategy that will at least guarantee some profits and limit the losses. There are a number of trading strategies that day traders can use, for instance swing trading, arbitrage trading, news trading among others.

c) Capital: One needs a lot of money to trade successfully. There is no guarantee that a day trader will make money by the end of the trading day, therefore day traders should be ready to risk a large amount of money in order to increase their chances of making a reasonable profit in the end. With significant capital, a day trader can capitalize well on intra-day price movements.

d) Discipline: Discipline is important in any kind of trade. Even with the best trading strategy, you may not succeed if you are not disciplined. You need to come up with your own trading criteria that you will always follow when trading. Many people lose money when they trade outside their plan. Day traders should always keep in mind that success is only possible if there is discipline.

Professional day traders are usually divided into two:

- Individual traders who work alone. They trade with their own money or they manage other people's money. They may not enjoy the privileges enjoyed by traders who work for larger institutions but they maintain strong ties with their brokers, which gives them access to important resource information and support.

- Those who work for large institutions. These enjoy various advantages, from a direct line to a dealing desk, large amounts of capital and leverage, expensive analytical software and much more. They trade for a living, therefore they are the ones who look for the slightest chance to make some profits and they react on any opportunity that presents itself even before individual traders think about it.

One needs access to some of the most important financial instruments and services in the market for successful day trading. Some of these are:

1. Access to multiple news sources: Information is definitely the most important trading tool. Gaining access to multiple sources of news ensures that you are well informed at all times and this will work in your favor when you are trading.

2. Access to the trading desk: This access is usually reserved for day traders that work for large institutions or those that deal with large amounts of money. The trading desk will give the traders order executions instantly for fast decision making. If you are smart enough, you can make a good trade by taking advantage of the differences in price before anyone else.

3. Access to analytical software: A trading software is a necessity for all day traders but it is quite expensive. Access to the software comes with a lot of benefits for the trader. You will not rely on news anymore since you

can analyze the market easily for yourself. The software has great features that makes day trading stress-free and increases chances of success. Some of the important features you get are:

- Automatic pattern recognition

- Broker integration

- Back testing

Day trading strategies

A trading strategy is the most important tool that a day trader has. Day traders will be closer to attaining success when they trade with a well-thought trading strategy. A strategy also ensures that they can minimize their risk. Here are some trading strategies that you can choose from to get started in day trading on the right footing:

1. Scalping: This is a very popular trading strategy in day trading. It involves making a trade almost immediately a trade becomes profitable even by a small margin. With this trading strategy, a trader does not have a specific price target. The price target become anything above the buying price.

2. The daily pivots: This strategy involves taking advantage of the daily market volatility. A trader using this strategy will aim at buying when the day's prices are down and sell when the prices go up. The target price is not specific here too. The trading opportunity comes when there is a slight sign of reversal.

3. Fading: This is the most risky and the most rewarding day trading strategy that a trader can go for. It involves shorting of stocks after prices start going up rapidly. There is no specific target price for this strategy too, but the right time to trade comes when the traders start stepping in. the prices can go up for a number of reasons, for instance when stocks have been overbought but this provides an opportunity for a trader to either buy or sell.

4. Momentum: A trader using this strategy will trade on news releases. The focus here is on the major trending moves that happen after a news release. One trader using this strategy will buy on news releases and hold onto the stocks until the market is favorable for selling. Another trader will sell on news release and wait for the prices to go down to buy.

Chapter 3:
Getting started in Day Trading

Day trading is a great way to make a living for traders who want to get involved in full time trading. It presents an opportunity for smart traders to make some money every day through trading. It is hard to tell just how much money one can make through day trading because there are so many external factors that come into play in making this determination.

However, truth of the matter is that many smart day traders trade full time. This is not the kind of trade you can get in if you do not have enough time on your hands. If you cannot carry out the trades yourself, then you will need to get a qualified and motivated person to do the day trading on your behalf. The only challenge one can expect if they want to trade full time is the uncertainty of the trade, which sometimes can become unbearable. One cannot always expect a steady income and this does not work really well for a lot of people. Nonetheless, these are minor issues that should not overwhelm you. Here is what you need to know to get started.

Learn the basics

Getting started in day trading is relatively simply. All that you need to get started is knowledge of the basics. Some of the things you need to study if you want to start smart in day trading are:

- General technical analysis

- Price action analysis

- Candle sticks

- Volume based analysis

- Trading strategies among others

In order to get prepared, you should take in a few online tutorials that can walk you through every step. In addition, ensure that you are familiar with all the terminology that you may encounter.

Practice

Once you have mastered the basics, start practicing. Trading simulators allow new day traders to trade on paper before they can get involved with actual trading. This is the perfect way to practice trading just to be sure that you know what you are doing when you start trading for real. Use the trading simulator to practice a few trading strategies and experience how they can be used in different kinds of stocks. By the time you start trading with real money, you will know what kind of strategy to use for a certain trade.

You also need to try trading in different kinds of systems too. There are websites these days that will allow you to practice day trading irrespective of whether the market is open or not. With good practice, you will know how to trade even before you start risking your money. This way, you can reduce your level of risk when you need to invest actual funds and wait for a return.

Save money

Day trading requires a good amount of money, therefore you have to set some money aside for the trade before you start trading. This is to ensure that you will have money to trade once you kick start trading. You need enough money for the minimum capital base that many trading platforms ask for and some leverage as well.

You will also need more money just in case you lose some in the trade, which happens all the time, so as to ensure that your minimum balance is maintained at all times. It is therefore important to have enough money for a start so as to minimize incidences where you will not trade. Since you are going to be taking risks when investing, make sure that the money you use for your investment is discretionary income. This way, even if you lose it, your day to day living will not be affected.

Shadow trading

When you have everything in place, you should consider shadow trading because it gives you an opportunity to see how a professional day trader trades. This can help you so much especially if you have never traded before. Sign up to a day trading chat room and meet professional day traders who have been in the trade for a very long time. They have the skills that you probably lack and with their experience, you can be sure that they trade better than anyone. By shadow trading, you allow yourself to see how things are done before you start trading and to copy some moves that professional day traders are making. Through this, you can start making money while you are still mastering some tricks and techniques that will give you a good chance to win on the live market.

Shadow trading is however quite risky and should be used sparingly. Sometimes prices change in just a few seconds and if you are not careful enough, you might make the wrong move especially if you are shadow trading. The person whose trades you are copying might be ahead of you and in just a few seconds, they could make a major profit while you are left picking up the crumbs left over. You always have to ensure that you are not too late to copy a move before you place your trade so as to avoid making a costly mistake.

Consider coaching

Many people have tried day trading without success and they lost a lot of money in the process. This is the reason why others are still skeptical about day trading. However, one can always learn what is needed first before they get involved and this can be possible if you consider coaching. There are professional coaches who are always willing to help out if you do not want to start by losing money in day trading. As has been mentioned earlier, this is a very tricky trade and one has to be absolutely sure and smart if they want to make a perfect move. Many people end up losing so much money even after learning everything there is in day trading but coaching will not let you down. You can get yourself a good day trading coach who will help you get to the next level and also help you identify and overcome of anything that can get in the way of your wining.

Chapter 4:
Risk Management

To be a successful day trader, you will have to learn and implement risk management. You should start by determining what risk is, how good and how bad it is. You should also know how to control risk to favor you and how risk management should be implemented as you trade.

Day traders should always have an exit strategy but many times most of them hold on to the losing trades with a hope that things will get better, but instead, they keep on losing. This is bad in so many ways, the most important ones being that it is a bad trading practice and again, it will affect your account balance. Risk management is all about learning how to stop these worst case scenarios like an expert. You need to know when to carry on and when to let go and this is how you successfully manage the risks involved in day trading. Here are some tips that can help a lot with risk management:

a) Set your stop orders

Every day trader must set a stop order regardless of the trading strategy that they are using. If you are selling, you should be able to exit the market if the price moves to a new high. Check your trading graph for a line of support or resistance and set a stopping order at that line. This should be determined mainly by the price action. If you are buying, you need to know when to stop buying, at least when the price hits a certain mark. Do not hold on hoping that things will take a sudden turn soon enough because this could lead to huge losses that could have been avoided in the first place.

b) Do not average down

When you already have a full position and it is already losing, adding to that position, even when you are trading according to your plan is not good for your trade. This always leads to huge losses that could have a great impact on your capital especially if you keep going on and the price is working against you. As explained above, you have to know when to stop. Averaging down will not work out well for any day trader because in most cases it results in a huge loss.

c) Only risk a certain percentage of your account balance.

The rule that day traders should abide in is not risking more than 1% of their total capital on one open trade, however promising it might be. Before you plan to risk per trade, you need to determine how much money you have in your account, then risk just a minimal percentage of it. Another day trading rule traders must follow is not having more than 15% of their account balance at risk at any given time. This means that if you happen to lose in all your trades, you will only lose about 15% of your capital, which is better than losing a higher percentage.

d) Know which stocks to trade in

There are weak stocks in bear markets and strong stocks traded in bull markets and you might be trading in all of them. You need to identify the strong stocks, which are those that are doing well in the market, so that you can always go for long trades in the strongest stocks when there is an uptrend in the market. When there is a downtrend on the other hand, go for short trades on the weaker stocks. This way, you will lose less in case of a loss and you can win big when there are profits. It will take an attentive and well informed day trader to make such a smart move at the right time.

e) Only trade when there is a trade setup

Following your trading plan and sticking to your trading strategy is crucial for day traders. If the market is not providing any trade setup that is based on your trading plan, you should not make a trade because you will be risking a lot. You should only trade when there is a set up that is in accordance to your trading plan. Remember that you do not have to trade every day. If a trading opportunity has not showed up, you can still trade the following day instead of making a regrettable move.

f) Minimize the stocks you trade in

Following too many stocks is not good if you want to manage your risk for better returns. Only go for the strongest stocks that you trade in the bull market and the weaker stocks that you trade in a bear market and you will be able to manage all of them well. This way, it will be easy for you to know when to trade and the stocks to trade when the market shifts to a certain direction.

Chapter 5:
Finding the Top Day Trading Picks

Making a successful move in day trading is very easy when you know how to trade and what to trade in. Even with the best trading strategies at hand, you will still not make the best move if you have not been able to apply the right strategy to the right stock during a trade. That is why many day traders fail, because they are unable to locate the best trading opportunities in the financial markets even when they have the right tools at hand.

The good news is that there is more than one way through which one can find the best trading picks for the day, and this presents a good trading opportunity for every day trader out there. This is in fact what traders need to know, because with the right opportunity, you can be sure of a profit, however small it can be.

Ideas from news reports

If you want to benefit from this, you have to read financial news reports every day. These are an excellent source of information because they are easily available. Through such reports, you will get to learn about specific companies that you can target during your trading sessions. Some trading platforms provide news reports for their traders. If not, you can always find this information online. Some of the aspects of reporting you should pay more attention to are:

- The earnings reports of companies that you could be interested in. This is a great determinant of whether the stock price will change or not.

- The new developments.

- The insider selling and buying of stocks.

These are some of the things that will determine the price change of a certain stock.

Alternatively, you can watch financial news on TV. There are financial news channels that you can capitalize in to get information on a daily basis on what is happening in the financial markets. The advantage of this is that you get the latest news reports, therefore it is easy to know what is moving the markets every minute for a chance to make a quick decision. You can also benefit from tips on stocks from financial experts especially if there is an expected significant price change in a stock of your interest.

Learning from other people

There are so many day traders in the world today and these are the people that should come to your mind once you decide to start day trading. Learning from other people about the trade and how to spot a good trading opportunity is better than learning from financial reports and online tutorials.

You can for instance join a group of people like you who want to start day trading or a group of people who have been day trading for a while. Even if it will cost you some money, it will be of great benefit to you considering the kind of advice that you can get from people who have been day trading for a long time and some of the tricks and tips that you can learn from them in the end. Once in that group, you can be sure that things that will benefit you will be discussed for instance some of the stocks to watch out for and this can give you an idea of when to trade for a profit.

Alternatively, you can follow people who are day trading in social media to get to know what they are up to and also to benefit from some of the ideas and advice that they might have for new day traders. The best people to follow in this case are professional and successful day traders who have been day trading for a long time. There are so many day traders today and their presence in social media makes it even better. They can share their trades in real time in these social sites for free and this is the kind of information that can give you a good idea on what stocks you should be watching out for in the next trade. You can also talk to them if you want for advice and insights on the same.

Ideas from your trading platform

Trading platforms provide every kind of support and information that traders will need when trading and this can benefit you so much. You can set up alerts for instance in order to be notified in case one of the most important signals that is in line with your trading philosophy and strategy indicate a change in the stock price. Many trading platforms have these technical signals and you can choose that which you feel are the most important in order to set a signal in case it is time for you to make a move. Once you receive a signal, it will be easy to know if you will trade or not depending on the trading strategy that you are using.

You can also use your trading platform to screen stocks. Most of the new trading platforms these days have a stock screener as one of the tools that you can use in order to search for stocks whose prices are likely to change, then you can get ready for the chance to place a trade. This is an important tool to use for new traders who have no idea where to get started in trading.

Trading platforms also provide reports pertaining to the stocks that are trending at a particular time for your decision making. Traders receive notifications at all times to let them know the stocks that are hot and those whose prices are likely to change as per a certain criteria. With such information at hand, you can easily weigh your options bearing in mind the kind of trading strategy that you are using so as to know when to trade and the stocks that you can trade in.

Chapter 6:
Trader Psychology

In hindsight, day trading appears easy, but in actual sense, it is a tough game that needs a lot of professionalism and discipline. Many people start day trading with high expectations but after a few trades, they realize that it is not working as they were expecting. A lot of emotions come into play and the emotions now makes things harder for the trader. That is why trading psychology is an important thing. You need to know how to control your emotions in order to trade like an expert for the benefits that day trading has to offer. Here are some psychological tactics that will help you trade like an expert:

1. Always remain calm: This will help especially when you are faced with a loss. A profit can also interfere with the way that you trade especially if it is a huge profit. Remain in a calm position at all times and try as much as you can to act according to your plan, not what your emotions dictate. Always have the worst case scenario in mind, so that you will know what to expect if things do not go the way you have planned. This will help you deal with your losses in a better and calmer way. In case of a loss, determine what went wrong so that you can be careful the next time you trade. Follow the plan to the latter irrespective of the outcome of the previous trade.

2. Always stick to the market that you have chosen and your preferred timeframes. Everything else in the market changes but you can control when and where you choose to trade. Your style should not change when you realize that you are not making profits as you had

planned. It is easier to learn day trading if you are able to maintain the same style throughout the trade.

3. Always act quickly and decisively: Immediately you come up with an informed decision to trade, that is when your price level have been reached and your trading requirements have been met, do it quickly enough. If you take some time, your trading opportunity could be missed and this could translate to a lost chance of making some profits. Acting slow does not work well for day traders. It can mean that all the efforts you have put in studying the market and following the trades have been for nothing.

4. Always work independently: This is the only way you can trade effectively. Do not call someone or email someone to find out if they think like you do about a certain trade. Your own instincts should be enough to convince you whether to place the trade or not. Relying on other people's opinions means that you are doubting yourself and this is not how a day trader should act. You should be able to trust that you have made the right calculations and that the decision that you will make will be the best.

5. Know yourself: Day trading has the potential to be a stressful affair; you have to be attentive and motivated at all times and this can elevate your levels of anxiety. You need to always be aware of your stress levels so that you can take a break once in a while to evaluate your priorities. This way, you will not be overwhelmed by trading, which can have a great impact on your life. Always know the position trading occupies in your life and remember what is important to you to minimize on the stress levels. You need to know that too much stress

will affect the way that you trade and this could lead to a loss and life complications. Once you hit a certain stress level, it could be time to take a break and come back when your mind is at ease.

6. Act deaf to other trader's opinions: d=Do not let the opinion of other traders influence the way that you trade. Other traders will always air their views and offer advice but you have to stick to your trading method and strategy if you want to trade like an expert. Stick to your time frames and your stops and follow your trading system and style to the end. Discipline will always come with amazing rewards that you do not want to miss. Trust your research and your instinct, and if you are tempted to take advice from someone else, ensure that it is backed up with solid facts.

7. Be flexible: Do not be too rigid in your positions. Some flexibility will help a lot in day trading. Market conditions change all the time, therefore you have to be flexible in your approach if you do not want to lose big. A smart trader is one that is able to adapt to market changes at all times and to act fast enough before they start losing. You should trade with an open mind at all times.

8. Patience will pay off soon enough: There is always the need for patience when day trading. If you are not able to find any trading opportunities at a certain time, do not force it; wait for the right chance and wait patiently. New traders will find themselves in such situations from time to time but as you learn the market better, you will realize that determining the right time to place a trade will be a lot easier. Experienced traders have better intuition and they can tell when to place a trade

and when not. It takes some time, therefore do not rush it.

Chapter 7:
Day Trading Secrets for Beginners

Holding a position for a short period of time is a tricky thing especially if you are an ambitious trader. Many traders need enough time to make the best decisions but day traders only have a few hours to lose their positions and ensure that they have gained something by the end of the day. This is what makes day trading a very tricky affair and many beginners may find it hard to enjoy some profits but it is not all that complicated.

You only need to learn one simple strategy that is rule based in order to be able to anticipate your moves correctly. Every trader needs some tricks and secrets that can increase their chances of making the right prediction for some profits, and day traders are not exceptional. As a beginner, these secrets will come in handy and they can help you start trading smart:

1. The best entry points that you have in day trading are scenarios where the supply and the demand are extremely imbalanced. Just like everything else in life, when the supply is down and there is still a high demand, the prices will definitely go up and if there is a high supply but less demand, the prices will definitely go down. The financial market is just like what happens in real life situations. These are therefore the turning points that day traders should always be on the lookout for in order to make a smart move in the end. You can easily know how the situation is from the price chart of even by studying historical examples from previous financial statements.

2. Do not lose your patience. Many successful day traders trade only when they see an opportunity to make some money, not every day. Beginners may be in a rush to trade for some small profits but this is what increases their chances of losing. Many beginners also think that the more they trade, the higher their chances of making some money, which is not always the case in day trading.

    If you want to be a smart trader, wait patiently or the best trading opportunity to present itself and strike for the profits. What many new traders do not know is that they should only trade when an opportunity that meets their trading criteria presents itself. You do not have to go against your best judgment just so as to get something small, which could result into a major loss. The best way to trade is to plan your trades well, then trade the plan.

3. Do not jump in before you set a price target. Many traders do not have a solid plan of trading and this is what results to so many fails in day trading. If you are planning to hold a long position in day trading, you have to make a decision beforehand pertaining to how much profits you will accept and any stop loss level that you can accept in case the trade does not favor you. You don't just make the decision but stick to it to the end. This way, your losses will be limited and chances of losing more than you can take becomes less. This trick will also help you keep your greed at bay especially when the price goes beyond your expectations. Once you have attained your initial target, you can now set a new target especially if you are trading in a strong market.

4. Learn from your experiences: It is almost impossible to trade in day trading without any losses. Many traders experience losses almost every day and instead of taking it personally and beating yourself up when this happens, you should take that as an opportunity to make a better judgment the next time you will be trading.

    Things will not always go your way in day trading but if you have followed the rules correctly and you have stuck to your trading strategy, you should know that you have done your best. Accepting losses and moving on to another trade will help you learn the tricks easily and you might start trading like an expert in no time at all.

5. When setting your targets, try a risk-reward ratio of 3:1. One of the best ways to trade in stocks is to set targets so as to work hard to meet those targets by the end of the trading period. Beginners in stock trading do not know how to do this too well, but you can start on the best foot if you understand the proper risk-reward ration to go for. Whenever you are setting targets, you need to think of losing and gaining and these should always go hand in hand because they happen at almost the same rate. If there are no gains, there will definitely be a loss.

    Setting a good target ratio is a good thing because it gives you a chance to win more of there is a win and lose less if there will be a loss. Traders trading on many trades do not have to go at a loss by the end of the trading period if they have set the right target ratios even when they lose in almost all their trades. They will only lose a small amount of money and gain so much in the few successful trades they have made that day.

6. Never limit day trading to stocks only. Many day traders do this and they deny themselves the chance to experience other securities that might work even better for them. Futures, forex and options are just like stocks; they display the same kind of volatility and liquidity therefore they might also be idea for day trading. You can consider them especially on those days when the stocks are not doing well in order to make something good out of your investments.

7. Never hesitate to push the order button. Many new day traders will hesitate to hit the order button even when they are sure that the opportunity is right. If you do not act quickly when the opportunity presents itself, you might miss the chance to make a profit.

Chapter 8:
Day Trading Mistakes to Watch Out For

Day trading is not really easy for beginners but today, with high speed internet connections and some confidence, anyone can day trade. There is a lot of information out there too, which is helping potential day traders to start day trading without too much hassle. Day trading involves a lot of risks and it is challenging as well, which is why you need to avoid making mistakes that could cost you a lot of money in the end. Here are some common mistakes day traders make and how you can overcome them for a smooth trade:

1. Unrealistic expectations: This is common to new day traders. High expectations are caused by a lot of things and they bring all manner of problems to you in the end. It is normal for a trader to expect that the market will move according to his desires and trading direction, but this does not happen all the time. You need to accept the fact that the market is not logical, therefore it does not know what you want. That is why you need a plan; come up with a good trading plan and trade with it. You should always be aware of the worst case scenarios so that it will not come as a surprise in case you lose.

2. Risking more: Successful day trading is all about risking but this does not mean that you should risk more capital. Traders should only risk the amount of money that they are ready to lose. What you need to know is that excessive risk does not translate to high returns. Risking large amounts of your capital means that you might lose so much money on one single trade. Professional traders risk less than 15% of their capital

on a single trade, which is a smart move. Risking less in a day means that your account will not be significantly affected in a single day and this will keep you trading for long.

3. Trading immediately after news: News affects the market significantly. Immediately the news are announced, the market starts moving aggressively, and some people try to take advantage of these moves to make some profits. This is a bad idea because chances of making huge losses are usually high when the prices are going up and down simultaneously. Smart day traders will wait for market volatility to subside in order to make a smart move. You need to trade when there is a definitive trend in the market and this is usually way after the news announcement.

4. Trading without a plan: Day trading is a business endeavor, just like every other business, therefore you need to start off with a trading plan. A trading plan will be like a map for you, to guide you through the trade at all times. This should be the most important tool you will use every day of your trading so that you will not trade outside the plan, which comes with some repercussions. You need to state one trading strategy that you will always use. In your trading plan, you need to define your trading edge, which is the right time to place your trade. You need to identify your trading metrics as well, which will tell you if you are trading successfully or not. You should include the kinds of stocks that you will be trading in as well as your exit strategy

5. Trading without sufficient education: To be a successful day trader, you need to have sufficient education and

experience. The best way to learn day trading is getting enough screen time and this means spending more time trading on screen and analyzing real time markets. This is what helps a trader to develop trading instincts, which help a lot when one is day trading. To be an expert trader, you have to invest some money and a lot for time to the trade. This is the only way you will be a successful professional day trader. Do not start trading and expecting to make huge profits on your first few trades. Trade for profits only when you master everything there is about day trading.

6. Overtrading: Trading over and over again in one day is a huge mistake that many day traders make. Smart traders only make one or two trades, then they take a break to trade later. Some days they do not even trade again after those trades. You have to be super selective and only trade those trades that seem highly prospective, and not every other trade that comes your way. That is why you should always trade as per your plan at all times, even when so many trading opportunities show up. The mistake many traders make is to start trading more when they realize that they have started attaining success. Instead of trading more, you can increase your trading size on the small trades that you make for higher returns.

Conclusion

There is a very strong belief that day trading is a hard skill to master, which is not necessarily the case. It may be tough at the beginning but it gets better as you go on mastering the skills and gaining experience. Many people have tried it in the past and probably failed in it because they did not take time to learn the necessary skills and to acquire the most required experience to trade successfully. Trading like an expert will take time but this does not mean that a new day trader will not make it.

There are many things that come into play for one to day trade successfully, and one of them is changing the way one thinks. One should be aware of how they have been programmed to think, and with the information out there about day trading and the stock market, you can easily change your thinking in order to grasp a trading opportunity for a profit.

Planning is another thing that traders need to embrace in order to trade successfully. Many traders have the belief that trading more amounts to more profits which is not always the case with day trading. A plan will help you concentrate on quality trades and not on quantity trades, with the former more beneficial than the latter.

Above all, learn as much as you can. There is a lot of information out there that you can take advantage of. Information is power and this will help you to trade successfully at all times.

www.ingramcontent.com/pod-product-compliance
Lightning Source LLC
Chambersburg PA
CBHW070426190526
45169CB00003B/1435